Candy Making
for Kids

Courtney Dial Whitmore

Photographs by Zac Williams

GIBBS SMITH
TO ENRICH AND INSPIRE HUMANKIND

*To my brother, David, for teaching me
the love of all things sweet!*

Manufactured in Shenzhen, China, in November 2012 by Toppan

The cooking and baking activities suggested in this book may involve the use of sharp objects and hot surfaces. Parental guidance is recommended. The author and publisher disclaim all responsibility of injury resulting from the performance of any activities listed in this book. Readers assume all legal responsibility for their actions.

First Edition
16 15 14 13 12   5 4 3 2

Published by
Gibbs Smith
P.O. Box 667
Layton, Utah 84041

1.800.835.4993 orders
www.gibbs-smith.com

Designed by Jennifer Barry Design
Printed and bound in China

Gibbs Smith books are printed on either recycled, 100% post-consumer waste, FSC-certified papers or on paper produced from sustainable PEFC-certified forest/controlled wood source. Learn more at www.pefc.org.

Library of Congress Cataloging-in-Publication Data

Whitmore, Courtney Dial.
   Candy making for kids / Courtney Dial Whitmore ; Photographs by Zac Williams. — 1st ed.
      p. cm.
   ISBN 978-1-4236-3022-7
1. Candy. I. Title.
TX791.W465 2012
641.85'3—dc23
                    2012006753

Acknowledgments

Thank you to Hollie Keith, Dan Moench and the entire Gibbs Smith team for all your hard work. Thank you to my mom, Phronsie, for your continued dedication to the love of entertaining and for the countless hours you spent helping me perfect these recipes. You are a dream stylist! Thank you to Chris and Henry for your support and love. A final thanks to the thousands of loyal and dedicated PIZZAZZERIE.com readers who continue to support me and my love of entertaining!

Contents

Introduction   6

Holiday Candies

Candy Cane Sled   9

Rudolph the Reindeer Pops   10

Silly Snowmen   13

Coconut Snowballs   14

Peppermint Ornament Wreaths   17

Spooky Halloween Ghosts   18

Candy Corn   21

Valentine's Conversation Hearts   22

Easter Baskets   25

Easter Bunny Pops   26

Candy Favorites

Peppermint Patties   29

Peanut Butter Bites   30

Gummies   33

Kids' Toffee   34

Candy Bar Truffles   37

S'more Truffles   38

Colorful Lollipops   41

Almond Rocky Road Bites   42

Sweet Creations

Crazy Caterpillars   45

Bird Nests   46

Bird Eggs   47

Seashell Pearls   48

Candy Pizza   51

Party Favorites

Candy Paints   52

Candy Play Dough   55

Candy Necklaces   56

Rainbow Sprinkle Fudge   59

Marshmallow Pops   60

Banana Split Bites   61

Sugared Rose Petals   62

Resources   64

Introduction

One of my fondest childhood memories was bike riding with my brother to a small candy store around the corner from our home in downtown Charleston, South Carolina. Picking out my favorite lollipop or piece of fudge to bring home and savor nibble by nibble was such a sweet treat as a child. I have always had an affinity for all things sweet (so much so that I affectionately deemed my maternal grandmother "Sweet"). So I'm excited to share these 30 candy recipes designed with kids in mind.

None of these recipes require the use of a candy thermometer and all of them are friendly for kids of all ages. Allow your children to enjoy the creating process as well as the sweet finish!

Helpful Hints for Candy Making

Tips on Tools

- A heavy, aluminum saucepan is essential for even heating.
- A jelly roll pan is the perfect pan for spreading out candies while cooling.
- Stainless steel cutters work well for making lollipops, cutting out chocolate, etc.
- A long-handled wooden spoon is a must-have for stirring candy.
- Parchment paper is a must-have, especially for making lollipops as they peel right off the parchment paper.
- Wax paper is another great must-have as it can be used to layer candies to avoid sticking.

Tips on Ingredients

- Always use pasteurized egg whites for safe eating.
- Buy the best chocolate you can for the best taste. When melting chocolate in a microwave, heat it in 15-second intervals between stirring.

Tips on Packaging

Homemade gifts are the **best** gifts, and that includes how they're presented too! Packing up sweet treats in cute ways is a must.

- Kids can get involved by wrapping boxes filled with candies in simple white or kraft paper. Add a painted handprint or children's artwork directly on the package!
- Think outside the "box" and try packaging candies in cellophane bags, mason jars, coffee mugs, tin cans, etc.
- Bows are my favorite! Whether they're natural raffia or bold grosgrain, bows add that finishing touch to any gift.

Candy Cane Sled

1 graham cracker cookie

2 ounces white chocolate bark

2 regular-sized candy canes

$1/8$ cup sweetened coconut

candies to decorate (gumdrops, peppermints, red hots, etc.)

Trim down a full graham cracker cookie in half for a small sled (2 $1/2$ x 2 $1/2$ inches) or cut down only a small amount for a medium sled (2 $1/2$ x 4 inches). Melt white chocolate bark coating in microwavable bowl until smooth. Dip graham cracker cookie (sled) into melted white chocolate until coated on both sides. Place white sled on top of 2 candy canes. Sprinkle sled with sweetened coconut. Decorate sleds with a variety of holiday candies (gumdrops, peppermints, red hots, etc.).

Rudolph the Reindeer Pops

chocolate bark

2-inch and 2 1/2-inch circle cutters

lollipop sticks or paper straws

mini pretzels

red hots, gum drops and peppermint candies for decorating

candy eyes

Christmas ribbon for bows

Line a cookie sheet with parchment paper. Melt 4 ounces of chocolate bark in a heatproof bowl in the microwave at 15-second intervals, stirring well between intervals until smooth. Pour chocolate into the circle cutters that were place on the parchment paper. Fill about 1/2-inch of chocolate into each circle cutter. Allow chocolate to cool for 2 to 3 minutes and then remove cutters. The chocolate will spread just a little. Push the lollipop stick (or paper straw) into the chocolate and twist to coat with the chocolate. Place 2 pretzels at the top of the reindeer's head for antlers. Add a nose and eyes. Let lollipops harden for about 30 minutes before removing from the cookie sheet.

Silly Snowmen

4 egg whites, room temperature

1 cup sugar

1 teaspoon vanilla extract

1 teaspoon cream of tartar

Preheat oven to 225 degrees F. Beat egg whites until stiff and peaks form. Add sugar, vanilla extract and cream of tartar. Continue to beat for about 4 minutes until very stiff. Fill plastic Ziploc bag with meringue mixture. Line a cookie sheet with parchment paper. Use a pen to draw 3 different sizes of circles ($1\,^1/_2$, 2 and $2\,^1/_2$ inches) for the snowman's body. Cut a corner in the plastic bag and pipe the meringue mixture onto the drawn circles, lifting up as you pipe. Spray your finger with non-stick cooking spray and carefully flatten the tips of the circles so they can be stacked later. Bake for 40 minutes. Turn off oven and let circles sit for an extra 15 minutes (do not open oven). Remove from oven and let cool.

Sweet Tip: Use frosting or melted white chocolate as glue to stick together the head, middle and body of the snowman. Create fun scarves, hats, eyes, etc., out of candies. For example, use fruit roll-ups to make scarves.

Coconut Snowballs

2 cups powdered sugar

$2/3$ cup sweetened condensed milk

1 teaspoon vanilla extract

1 teaspoon almond extract

$1/2$ teaspoon salt

3 cups flaked coconut

Mix powdered sugar, condensed milk, extracts and salt together until well combined. Stir in 1 cup of coconut and mix well. If dough is too stiff, add a little more condensed milk. Shape into 1-inch snowballs and roll in remaining 2 cups of coconut. Store snowballs in an airtight container in the refrigerator.

Peppermint Ornament Wreaths

Makes 20 wreaths

1 (18-ounce) bag round
    peppermint hard candies

decorating: red hots, gumdrops,
    M&M's, etc.

royal icing or melted white
    chocolate bark as glue

Christmas ribbons and bows for
    hanging on the tree

Line a cookie sheet with parchment paper. Remove the wrappers from the peppermints. Arrange 5 peppermints in a circle on the paper. Cook at 300 degrees F for
6 minutes. These candies melt quickly, so watch carefully not to let them stay too
long or they will be a solid round piece of peppermint. Remove candies from oven.
Cool and remove from the cookie sheet. Attach a circle of ribbon to peppermint
and add a bow, and they are ready to hang on your tree! Be careful because the
candy is thin and can break easily.

Spooky Halloween Ghosts

$1/2$ cup (1 stick) butter, room
temperature

1 (7-ounce) jar marshmallow fluff

1 pound powdered sugar

2 tablespoons black frosting

Mix together butter, marshmallow fluff and powdered sugar in electric mixer. Beat until smooth. Add more powdered sugar until soft, moldable texture forms. Mold ghost shapes with hands or fill into large plastic bag, cut corner and pipe out ghost shapes. Add eyes and mouth with black frosting.

Candy Corn

Makes 50–60 candy corn

1 (10-ounce) bag miniature marshmallows

1 1/2 pounds powdered sugar

1/4 cup shortening

yellow and red food coloring

Melt entire bag of marshmallows with 3 tablespoons of water in a microwavable bowl in 30-second intervals until completely smooth. Stir in 3 cups powdered sugar until dough begins to form. Rub hands over shortening and begin to knead the marshmallow fondant. Powder a flat surface with powdered sugar. Knead fondant on flat surface and continue to add remaining powdered sugar until smooth and not sticky. Divide into 3 balls (small, medium, large). Flatten 1 and add yellow food coloring. Roll and knead until the coloring spreads evenly across ball. Repeat with second ball and a combination of yellow and red food coloring to create orange. Arrange balls from large to small sizes and form into triangle shape.

Sweet Tip: Vary the colors for other holidays such as pink for Valentine's Day or green for St. Patrick's Day!

Valentine's Conversation Hearts

Makes 25 conversation hearts

$1\frac{1}{4}$ teaspoons unflavored gelatin

$\frac{1}{4}$ cup water

1 teaspoon light corn syrup

$\frac{1}{2}$ teaspoon almond or vanilla extract

red food coloring

4 cups powdered sugar

edible markers

Place gelatin, water and light corn syrup into a heatproof bowl. Stir until well dissolved and then microwave for 30 seconds. Pour into mixing bowl and add the extract and 5 drops of red food coloring. Add 1 cup powdered sugar and beat with electric mixer. Continue to add powdered sugar, 1 cup at a time, mixing well after each addition. Mixture will change from a wet liquid form to stiff, sticky dough. Knead the dough using extra powdered sugar if needed.

Place on a powdered sugar surface and roll out to $\frac{1}{4}$ inch thick. Using $2\frac{1}{2}$-inch or 3-inch heart-shaped cookie cutter, cut out hearts using all the dough. Let hearts air dry overnight. Use edible markers to write messages and then package in fun containers.

For Younger Kids: Parents can make this recipe fun for little ones by creating the hearts ahead of time and then letting the kids decorate the hearts.

Easter Baskets

1 envelope unflavored gelatin

$1/4$ cup water

2 teaspoons light corn syrup

4 cups powdered sugar

food coloring

marshmallow twisted rope candy

4-inch scalloped or round cutters

Easter grass

candy eggs

Easter ribbon

Place gelatin, water and corn syrup in a heatproof bowl. Stir until dissolved and then microwave for 30 seconds. Pour into a mixing bowl and add food coloring. Lavender, pink and yellow are great colors to use at Easter. Add 1 cup powdered sugar and beat until mixed. Continue adding the powdered sugar, one cup at a time, until it is all used. Knead dough using extra powdered sugar if needed. Place on a powdered sugar surface and roll out to $1/4$ inch thick. Using a 4-inch scalloped or round cutter, cut out the baskets. Lay each circle over a small custard bowl sprayed with Pam. Adjust the shapes and let dry overnight. The next day turn baskets right side up and glue handles in place with melted bark or royal icing. Add a little Easter grass, candy eggs and a bow on the handle and you have a fun candy basket.

Easter Bunny Pops

Makes 8 Pops

1 bag large marshmallows
  (campfire size works really well)

granulated sugar

1 bag gummy fish (yellow and
  orange)

assorted jelly beans

candy eyes

16 ounces white bark coating

8 lollipop sticks or striped straws

Easter ribbon for bows

2 1/2-inch round cutters

Use kitchen scissors to cut marshmallows in half and then cut each circle into 2 pieces shaped like crescent moons. These are the bunny ears. After cutting 16 ears, roll each ear in granulated sugar and place on parchment paper to dry. Use scissors to cut the gummy fish into 3-inch-long pieces of gummy. Each bunny will need 6 pieces of long gummy to be the whiskers. Eight bunnies will need 48 whiskers. Jellybeans will be the noses and can also be used as eyes instead of candy eyes. Line a cookie sheet with parchment paper. Melt 4 ounces of bark at a time in a microwave bowl at 15-second intervals until melted. Place the cutters on the parchment paper. Pour the bark into the cutters about 1/2 inch deep. Allow bark to cook for 3 or 4 minutes and then remove cutters. The bark will spread slightly. Push a lollipop stick or straw into the bark and twist to coat the stick. Push 2 marshmallow ears in the top of the lollipop, a jellybean nose, 3 whiskers on each side and 2 candy eyes. Let harden on the parchment paper for about 30 minutes. Embellish with a ribbon. Lollipops can be made earlier and then decorated. If made early, melt a little bark and have in a bowl to use as glue for decorating.

Peppermint Patties Makes 48 patties

$^{1}/_{4}$ cup pasteurized egg whites

1 (16-ounce) box powdered sugar

$^{1}/_{2}$ teaspoon salt

$^{1}/_{8}$ teaspoon lemon extract

$^{1}/_{2}$ teaspoon peppermint extract

1 drop liquid red food coloring

Beat egg whites and powdered sugar until dough forms. Add salt, extracts and food coloring. Knead dough until soft and smooth. If dough is too dry, add $^{1}/_{2}$ teaspoon of water until smooth consistency. Form 1-inch balls and lay on wax or parchment paper dusted with powdered sugar. Dip fork in powdered sugar, shake off excess and flatten ball with fork to form indention. Let air dry for 1 hour.

Sweet Tip: Instead of creating balls with dough, roll out dough with rolling pin and kids can cut out peppermint patties using small shaped cookie cutters. Or try jazzing them up by dipping dried peppermint patties in white or milk chocolate and sprinkle with crushed peppermint, sprinkles, etc.

Peanut Butter Bites Makes 48 bites

$1/2$ cup butter, melted

$1^1/4$ cup peanut butter

1 (16-ounce) box powdered sugar

$1/2$ teaspoon vanilla extract

$1/2$ teaspoon salt

coatings: mini chocolate chips,
    toffee pieces, sprinkles, etc.

Cream butter and peanut butter with electric mixer until well blended. Add powdered sugar, 1 cup at a time, mixing well between each addition. Add vanilla extract and salt and mix well. Roll dough into 1-inch balls and then roll in a variety of fun candies such as mini semi-sweet chocolate chips, toffee pieces, sprinkles, etc. Store bites in airtight container in refrigerator.

Gummies

1 cup water

2 (3-ounce) packages Jell-O,
  any flavor

$1/2$ teaspoon Kool-Aid, any flavor

2 envelopes unflavored gelatin

Spray an 8 x 8-inch pan with non-stick cooking spray. You can also use molds to make fun shapes; just spray non-stick cooking spray in the molds. Place water in small saucepan over medium-high heat. Bring to a boil and immediately add Jell-O, Kool-Aid and gelatin. Stir vigorously until everything is dissolved. Pour into the pan (or molds) and place in refrigerator for 20 minutes. Remove and cut into fun shapes with cookie cutters.

Kids' Toffee

Makes 65-70 pieces

28–29 squares honey graham
    crackers

1 cup light brown sugar

1 cup (2 sticks) butter

1 (12-ounce) package semi-sweet
    chocolate chips

1 cup regular (or mini) M&M's

Preheat oven to 350 degrees F. Line a jelly roll pan with aluminum foil and spray with non-stick cooking spray. Spread honey graham crackers until pan is full to all sides. Combine brown sugar and butter in saucepan over medium-high heat. Bring to a rolling boil and remove from heat. Pour over layer of graham crackers and spread until evenly coated. Bake for 10 minutes. Remove and pour package of chocolate chips over whole pan. As chocolate melts, use back of spoon to spread chocolate to all sides. Sprinkle with M&M's. Allow toffee to cool for 1 to 2 hours or until firm. Break into bite-size pieces.

Candy Bar Truffles

8 ounces cream cheese, room temperature

$1/4$ cup butter, melted

1 package Oreos, crushed

$1/4$ teaspoon salt

$1 1/2$ cups powdered sugar

1 regular-size candy bar (Kit Kat or Snickers)

2 cups (16 ounces) semi-sweet chocolate chips

2 tablespoons vegetable oil

Beat cream cheese and butter until combined. Add Oreos, salt and powdered sugar and mix well. Cut candy into $1/2$ inch pieces. Take 1 piece of candy and form a ball around it with the Oreo mixture. Place on a parchment lined cookie sheet. Continue making candy bar truffles until all ingredients are used. Refrigerate balls for 20 minutes. Melt chocolate with vegetable oil in the microwave. Dip chilled balls into melted chocolate until coated. Using 2 forks to hold the ball works well. Place chocolate coated balls on parchment paper. Let harden and store in an air tight container in the refrigerator.

S'more Truffles

$1/3$ cup heavy cream

$1/2$ teaspoon salt

$1/2$ teaspoon vanilla extract

2 cups semi-sweet chocolate chips

2 tablespoons vegetable oil

20 miniature marshmallows

$1^1/2$ cups graham crackers
   (roughly crushed)

Combine cream, salt and vanilla extract in a large bowl. Melt chocolate and vegetable oil in a heatproof microwave bowl at 15-second intervals, stirring after each interval until it is melted. Stir melted chocolate into the cream mixture. Pour into a parchment-lined 8 x 8-inch pan and refrigerate for 1 hour. Scoop out a tablespoon of chocolate and wrap around a marshmallow. Roll in the graham cracker bites and place on a cookie sheet. After making all the truffles, store in an airtight container in the refrigerator.

Colorful Lollipops

25 round peppermints, Jolly Ranchers or other hard candies

5 white lollipop sticks

red hots, gum drops, M&M's, jelly beans, etc., for decorating the lollipops

white bark or royal icing as glue

Remove wrappers from hard candy pieces. Place on a cookie sheet lined with parchment paper. Arrange 5 peppermints in a circle. The Jolly Ranchers can be 2 side-by-side wide and 2 deep, using 4 Jolly Ranchers for 1 lollipop. Only arrange 4 lollipops on 1 cookie sheet, allowing for the candies to melt and spread out. Heat the oven to 300 degrees F and bake for 6 minutes. As soon as candy comes out of the oven, push a stick into it before candy hardens. Use melted white bark or royal icing as glue to decorate the lollipops.

Almond Rocky Road Bites

Makes 3–4 dozen (40 pieces)

1 1/2 pounds Hershey's chocolate
bars with almonds

1/2 cup chunky peanut butter

1 cup dry roasted almonds,
chopped

1 1/2 cups Rice Krispies cereal

1 cup miniature marshmallows

Melt chocolate bars in heatproof bowl in a microwave at 15-second intervals. Stir in peanut butter and mix until smooth. Combine nuts and cereal in a large bowl. Pour chocolate mixture over cereal mixture and mix well. Stir in miniature marshmallows. Drop by teaspoon onto a cookie sheet lined with wax paper. Let cool and set for 1 hour in the refrigerator.

Crazy Caterpillars

3 cups Rice Krispies cereal

2 tablespoons butter, melted

1 teaspoon salt

2 cups miniature marshmallows (or 20 regular-size marshmallows)

candy eyes, hard candies, mini M&M's and pretzels

Pour cereal in a large bowl. Melt butter and salt in a medium saucepan over medium-high heat. Add marshmallows and stir with wooden spoon until melted and smooth. Pour marshmallow mixture over cereal and stir well. Use hands (spray with non-stick spray to prevent sticking) to form 40 1-inch balls. Combine 4 krispie balls to make each caterpillar. Use candy eyes, hard candies, M&M's and pretzels to make caterpillar eyes, faces and feet.

Bird Nests

1 tablespoon vegetable oil

1 (11-ounce) package butterscotch
   chips (or peanut butter chips)

$1/2$ teaspoon salt

1 cup peanuts

1 large can (2 cups) chow mein
   noodles

Combine vegetable oil, butterscotch chips and salt in a microwaveable bowl. Melt at 30-second intervals until smooth. Combine nuts and noodles in a medium bowl. Pour melted butterscotch over nuts and noodles and stir well to coat. Spray hands with non-stick cooking spray to make it easier to mold nests from the mixture. Working quickly, form 2-inch nests while the mixture is still warm and then lay on a cooking sheet lined with parchment or wax paper. Allow to cool and then peel off paper.

Bird Eggs

4 ounces cream cheese, softened

1 (16-ounce) package powdered sugar

3 drops blue liquid food coloring

1 drop yellow liquid food coloring

1 teaspoon vanilla extract

$^1/_2$ teaspoon almond extract

$^3/_4$ cup finely chopped toasted pecans

$^1/_2$ cup granulated sugar

Beat cream cheese, powdered sugar, food coloring and extracts until dough forms. Knead in pecans until mixed well. Form 1-inch oval-shaped eggs and roll in sugar. Allow to set on parchment paper or store in airtight container until ready to use.

Seashell Pearls

4 ounces cream cheese, softened

1 (16-ounce) package powdered
    sugar

1 teaspoon vanilla extract

$1/2$ teaspoon almond extract

pearl disco dust

Beat cream cheese, powdered sugar and extracts until dough forms. Form $1/2$ to
1-inch balls. Use a paintbrush to tap disco dust on balls for a pearl shimmer. Allow
to set on parchment paper or store in an airtight container until ready to use.

Candy Pizza

1 cup sweetened flake coconut	red gum drops
red and yellow food coloring	black licorice
1 jar red maraschino cherries	16 ounces white bark coating
1 jar green maraschino cherries	3- and 4-inch cutters

Place coconut in a bowl. Add 2 drops of yellow and 1 drop of red food coloring on the coconut and stir until it resembles cheese. You may have to add a little more food coloring if needed. Open and drain the red and green cherries. Place green cherries on a cutting board and slice to make circles. Cut red cherries into small pieces. Place a red cherry piece into the center of a green cherry. These cherries will look just like pimiento-stuffed olives. Slice red gum drops, making small round pieces that will be pepperoni slices. Cut black licorice into tiny pieces to look like chopped black olives. Microwave 4 ounces of white bark in a heatproof bowl at 15-second intervals, stirring after each interval. Continue doing this until the bark is melted. Place parchment paper on a cookie sheet and then place the cutters on the paper. Pour melted bark into each cutter until about $1/2$ inch deep. Let bark harden for 3 or 4 minutes and then remove the cutters. The bark will spread out just a little. Sprinkle with coconut (cheese) and place the green olives and pepperoni around the pizza. Sprinkle the black olives. The pizzas are ready to serve.

Candy Paints

¼ cup powdered sugar

1 teaspoon pasteurized egg whites

4 drops food coloring

Mix powdered sugar, egg whites and food coloring in a bowl and stir well. Repeat steps with different colors of food coloring for a variety of paint colors. This paint works well on marshmallows, white chocolate, etc. Use candy molds, such as cars, filled with white chocolate. Then paint and enjoy!

Candy Play-Dough

8 ounces cream cheese, softened

2 (16-ounce) boxes powdered
sugar

food coloring (liquid or gel)

Beat cream cheese until creamy. Add in powdered sugar at 2-cup intervals until dough forms. Color with food coloring (or divide for multiple colors). Play-dough is edible. Play-dough can be stored in an airtight bag or container in the refrigerator for up to a week.

Candy Necklaces

10 yards $5/8$-inch-wide sheer
 ribbon for necklace

10 yards $3/8$-inch ribbon for
 decoration

gummy candies in variety of colors
 (Life Savers Gummies work
 great)

Each necklace needs one 36-inch length of the $5/8$-inch sheer ribbon. Cut the $3/8$-inch ribbon to 6 inches long. Each necklace needs 5 to 7 pieces of 6-inch ribbon. Ten yards of assorted designs will decorate 10 necklaces. Thread 1 of the 36-inch pieces of ribbon through a large gummy to the middle of the ribbon. Next, tie a 6-inch piece of ribbon on either side of the gummy. Thread a smaller gummy on either side of the ribbon and repeat. Necklaces are ready to wear, and enjoy nibbling if desired!

Rainbow Sprinkle Fudge

4 ounces cream cheese, room temperature

3 cups powdered sugar

$1/4$ teaspoon salt

1 (11-ounce) package white chocolate chips

1 teaspoon vanilla extract

1 teaspoon almond extract

$3/4$ cup rainbow sprinkles

Beat cream cheese until smooth and fluffy. Gradually add powdered sugar and salt. Melt white chocolate in microwavable bowl in 30-second intervals until smooth. Pour into cream cheese mixture and stir until blended. Stir in extracts. Pour in $1/2$ cup rainbow sprinkles—do not over-stir or sprinkles will become melted and muddy the color of fudge. Pour fudge mixture into 9 x 9-inch pan lined with wax paper. Sprinkle remaining $1/4$ cup rainbow sprinkles over top of poured fudge. Refrigerate until chilled and then cut into squares.

Marshmallow Pops

Makes 20 pops

20 large marshmallows

20 lollipop sticks

2 cups assorted candy melts or chocolate chips

sprinkles, candies, edible decorations

Line a jelly roll pan or baking sheet with wax paper. Insert lollipop sticks into marshmallows. Melt candy melts or chocolate chips in microwavable bowl at 15-second intervals until smooth, stirring well between each interval. Dip marshmallows into candy melts or chocolate until coated. Decorate with sprinkles and other edible decorations. Set on wax paper to cool.

Banana Split Bites

Makes 30 bites

12 ounces white bark coating

1 (6-ounce) bag banana chips

1 cup sweetened coconut

12 ounces chocolate bark coating

$1/4$ cup rainbow sprinkles

30 maraschino cherries

Melt white bark coating in microwavable bowl in 30-second intervals until smooth. Dip half of the banana chips into white bark coating and coat completely on both sides. Lay coated banana chips on layer of parchment paper. Sprinkle sweetened coconut on top of banana chips while coating is still wet so coconut sticks. Top with a second, uncoated banana chip. Melt chocolate bark coating in microwaveable bowl in 15-second intervals until smooth. Drizzle chocolate over second banana chip. Top chocolate layer with rainbow sprinkles. Finish with maraschino cherry.

Sweet Tip: When assembling Banana Split Bites, use extra white chocolate as "glue."

Sugared Rose Petals

Makes 20–25 sugared petals

2 rosebuds (just opening),
   organically grown

$1/2$ cup pasteurized egg whites

$1/2$ cup granulated sugar

To make sugared rose petals, use only organically grown roses (grown with no pesticides). Each rosebud will make about 10 to 15 petals. Carefully pull off petals, rinse and pat dry with paper towels. Dip each rose petal into small bowl of egg whites and then into sugar. Place sugared petals on parchment-lined cookie sheet to dry. Let dry at room temperature for 2 hours, then turn over petals and continue drying overnight. Store petals in an airtight container between layers of wax paper.

Resources

Sprinkles, Edible Decorations, Candy Making Supplies

bakeitpretty.com

sweetbakingsupply.com

layercakeshop.com

wilton.com

Packaging Resources

nashvillewraps.com

shopsweetlulu.com

papermart.com

bagsandbowsonline.com

Party & Holiday Entertaining Tips

pizzazzerie.com

With a love of entertaining and a background in marketing, **Courtney Dial Whitmore** has become a well-known stylist and blogger in the field of party design and entertaining. Her expertise has been seen in HGTV.com, *Nashville Lifestyles Magazine*, *Ladies Home Journal*, AOL's DIY *Life*, *Get Married Magazine*, MarthaStewart.com, and more. Also the author of *Push-Up Pops*, Courtney writes for Disney, *The Huffington Post*, *SHE KNOWS*, and additional lifestyle publications. She currently resides in Nashville, Tennessee, with her husband.

Photograph © Kate Whitmore Photography